From
Tabletop
to
Mountaintop

My Journey

BILL HILGEMANN

Fulton Books
Meadville, PA

Published by Fulton Books 2023

ISBN 979-8-88731-997-1 (paperback)
ISBN 979-8-88731-998-8 (digital)

Printed in the United States of America

The Beginning

"For My thoughts are not your thoughts, nor are your ways My ways," says the Lord. For as the heavens are higher than the earth, so are My ways higher than your ways, and My thoughts than your thoughts.

—Isaiah 55:8–9

Have you ever wondered how things can happen that do not seem even possible, especially at a certain point in someone's life? I am here to try to explain exactly how that happened to me. In order to make sense of this, I have to start from what I call *the beginning*.

I was just the average child growing up. We lived on the farm, Dad worked for a farmer, and we lived normally as I saw it. My brother and older sister and I would go to Sunday school with the neighbors. They would take us to church; then my parents would come and pick us up after Sunday school. My parents were never into the Lord or any part of the church. What amazes me though is I can remember watching *The Ten Commandments* every year on TV. There were drinking and lots of profanity growing up; that's for sure. Throughout my younger years, I went to many Bible studies, but I was not truly involved. It was more of a way to get out of the house for a while. We moved to Arapahoe, Colorado, in Aug. 1978, and it is a very small community. When I said it was a way to get out there, we took advantage by going to youth groups to get out.

As the years passed, I was blessed with two boys. My marriage did not work out, and I raised the boys with granny's help. During the years, I dealt with alcohol issues many times. It cost me a lot of money and a couple of jobs. I had lost my job due to a DUI, and I was home watching TV when the Lord spoke to me. I had recently moved my girlfriend and her daughter in with the boys and me. On *The 700 Club* that day, the word *fornication* came up, and I had never heard of that word before. Now my girlfriend and I had been going to church on a regular basis, and I was beginning to learn the Word.

That day when I heard the word *fornication* for the first time, the Lord took me to my bride and had me go to the book of Hebrews, I had a yellow highlighter, and He had me go through the book randomly. I highlighted many verses throughout that book. I did not think any more about it at the time. When my girlfriend got home from work, I told her and showed her what the Lord had done. So she went through and put the verses in order as I had highlighted them, and an amazing letter appeared. I call this letter *my letter from God*, and I have it in a frame, and it hangs on my wall to this day.

My Letter from God

For the earth which drinks in the rain that often comes
upon it, and bears useful herbs for those by whom
it is cultivated, receives blessing from God.
For if we sin willfully after we have received the knowledge
of the truth, there no longer remains a sacrifice for sins.
Therefore, strengthen the hands which hang down, and the feeble
knees, and make straight paths for your feet, so that when is lame
may not be dislocated, but rather be healed, and pursue peace with
all people, and holiness, with which no one will see the Lord.
See that you do not refuse Him who speaks. For if they did not
escape who refused Him who spoke on earth, much more shall we
not escape if we, turn away from Him who peaks from heaven.
Marriage is honorable among all, and the bed undefiled,
but fornicators and adulterers God will judge.
But do not forget to do good and to share, for
with such sacrifices God is well pleased.
Now may the God of peace who brought up our Lord Jesus from
the dead, that great Shepherd of the sheep, through the blood of
the everlasting covenant, make you complete in every good work
to do His will, working in you what is well pleasing in His sight,
through Jesus Christ, to whom be glory forever and ever. Amen.

I do not know the exact date when the Lord revealed it to me. It was the spring of 2002 though. After we both read it, we came to the understanding that we were sinning, and she moved out the next week.

Now fast forward to 2020, I am sitting in my chair, still drinking daily. I would start around 2:00 p.m. every day. I heard a still small voice in my conscience, and the Lord asked me how I will be able to drive my mom to the hospital if I am drunk. It was a slap in the face. I got up and dumped out the drink I had and all the alcohol I had in the house. I can honestly say I have not had another drink since that day. I have heard many times in my lifetime how alcohol is a disease and a family disease. I never could ever get the thought of alcohol out of my mind for probably forty years. That day when the Lord asked me that question, it opened my eyes. I now believe any kind of addiction is from the enemy; he wants to use every way possible to destroy us.

The fall of 2021 was the beginning of my journey. I worked in the oil field for many years and was used to waking up around 4:30 a.m. or 5:00 a.m. for many, many years. I do not know the exact date, but all of a sudden, one morning, I woke up at 3:00 a.m. I got up and walked around awhile, and I decided to go back to bed. The next morning, I woke up again around 3:00 a.m. This time I heard in my conscience to turn the TV on. I went to the history channel, and at 4:00 a.m., a show came on, and at 4:30 a.m., another one came on. The first one was called *Amazing Facts*; the second was *Turning Point*. I watched two days of these, and on the third day, David Jeremiah (*Turning Point* minister), spoke on how, when he was first beginning his ministry, the Lord had told him to write out Scripture. He said it was the best advice he had gotten.

On the fourth day, I went to my kitchen table, and the Lord had me start in Matthew. I began writing out the Word. I expect it will take me one and a half to two years to complete the whole Bible. I wrote through October, November, December, January, and most of February. I still continue writing every day as I write this. February is when the Lord began the next phase. It was about the time when Russia invaded Ukraine in February that the Lord had me start a journal. I spent February, March, and April listening to sermons on YouTube and watching the news from around the world. I was putting info in my journal as things were happening. I was not knowing, at the time, that the Lord was preparing for a journey I never knew was possible. And it involved me!

If we trust and obey, He will lead the way!

The Preparation

For the Lord gives wisdom, from His mouth come knowledge
and understanding. He stores up sound wisdom for the
upright. He is a shield to those who walk uprightly. He guards
the paths of justice, and preserves the way of His saints.

—Proverbs 2:6–8

As I began writing, I had no idea what or why I was writing all these verses and news info. On May 3, I got my first instruction from the Lord. I wrote and initiated it. He told me, "Feed My sheep!" I had no idea where the Lord was taking me. So I wrote in my journal the questions I was having in my thoughts. I asked, "Why me? Why start in Cheyenne Wells?"

On May 21, 2022, the Lord answered my questions. God told me, "You are no different from the ones I used in the earlier days. I created you for this time in My master plan. You are blessed. Get out, and feed My sheep! Don't get upset. You can't make anyone believe. Remember it is as in the days of Noah. People won't believe, but don't give up. Just plant the seed. I am the same yesterday, today, and forever. I never change. Why would this be any different from times past? I used men like you and will use men like you now to fulfill My kingdom!" Then over the next few days, He revealed Scripture to answer my questions.

> Surely the Lord God does nothing, unless He reveals His secret to His servants, the prophets. (Amos 3:7)

All these verses came to me, and the Lord had me write them in the very front of my journal so I would never forget why He chose me for this journey.

> All Scripture is given by inspiration of God, and is profitable for doctrine, for reproof, for correction, for instruction in righteousness, that the man of God may be complete, thoroughly equipped for every good work. (2 Timothy 3:16–17)

> Fear not, for I have redeemed you. I have called you by your name, you are Mine. (Isaiah 43:1)

> The Lord your God will be with you wherever you go. (Joshua 1:9)

> I, even I have spoken, yes, I have called him, I have brought him, and his way will prosper. (Isaiah 48:15)

> I will guide you with My eye. (Psalm 32:8)

> Behold, the former things have come to pass, and new things I declare, before they spring forth I tell you of them. (Isaiah 42:9)

> For you shall not go out with haste, nor go by flight. For the Lord will go before you, and the God of Israel will be your rear guard. (Isaiah 52:12)

> "You are My witnesses," says the Lord and My servant whom I have chosen that you may know

and believe Me, and understand that I am He.
(Isaiah 43:10)

As time went on, I continued to receive instructions from the Lord. This next section is the order of instructions as I received them. On May 3, the Lord told me, "Feed My sheep!" On May 15, He answered one of my questions referring to why I should start my journey in Cheyenne Wells. He told me that I need to start in my area (Cheyenne Wells) because so many people I know don't have a clue of what is coming. It's because the local teachers aren't telling them, and many don't know the truth themselves. On May 21, the Lord told me, "You are no different from the men I used in earlier days. I created you for this exact time. Don't get upset. You can't make anyone believe. Don't give up. Just plant the seeds."

As I was beginning to visit the local churches, I was still unaware of where this journey was headed. So while trying to explain to others what was happening to me, the Lord had me write,

> With men this is impossible, but with God all things are possible. (Matthew 19:26)

> Call unto Me, and I will answer thee, and show thee great and mighty things which thou knowest not. (Jeremiah 33:3)

> The Lord has appeared of old to me, saying, "Yes, I have loved you with an everlasting love, therefore with lovingkindness I have drawn you." (Jeremiah 31:3)

As I was doing my daily writing, on June 8, I was listening to a sermon on Jonah, and I had never heard it taught that way. I read it myself and understood that Jonah disobeyed what the Lord had told him to do. And the Lord had him swallowed up by a whale. The Lord told me, "Don't be like Jonah!" At that time in my journey, I still did not have a clue about what to do. The Lord had been hinting at an upcoming message to g—As the days passed, I was getting thoughts of a sermon. On June 15, the Lord told me, "Go to the beginning of the speech and inform the people how I have been preparing you (me) for this time in My plan and how I have been having you write out the Bible word by word and waking you up every morning to watch *Amazing Facts* and *Turning Point*. Now the end of days is near."

> And do this, knowing the time, that now it is high time to awake out of sleep, for now our salvation is nearer than when we first believed. (Romans 13:11)

> The Lord God has given me the tongue of the learned, that I should know how to speak a word in season to him who is weary. He awakens me morning by morning. He awakens my ear to hear as the learned. (Isaiah 50:4)

On June 18, I was still wondering where this was really headed, so the Lord had me write: "I am using you to accomplish My plan. Many people won't go to church because they are ashamed of their lifestyle. I need you to speak to them as a friend, not a minister."

On June 22, I wrote in my journal: "No matter what limitations you may have, God will use anyone who believes in Him to fulfill His purpose. He does not judge our ability by the world's standards but by His own abilities—which are limitless!" He also had me write on the twenty-second: "Be careful that a man not put his trust in another man's word. Only God has the answers. Trust in Him and His Word, the Holy Bible."

On June 24, I wrote: "I now understand how God moved men to write the Bible. As I have been going through this journey, I am inspired by God every day to do this book."

> My sheep hear My voice, and I know them, and they follow Me. (John 10:27)

Whether you have been with Him for many years or are just learning His ways, you can take heart because your tenderhearted Shepherd calls out to you in a way that you can recognize Him.

> But without faith it is impossible to please Him, for he who comes to God must believe that He is, and that He is a rewarder of those who diligently seek Him. (Hebrews 11:6)

> You will show me the path of life, in Your presence is fullness of joy. At Your right hand are pleasures forevermore. (Psalm 16:11)

> I have learned to be content in whatever circumstances I am. (Philippians 4:11)

As this journey continued, the Lord revealed many simple things to make this so much easier to accomplish. I was going to the local churches and sharing what was happening, and I was struggling with finding various verses and memos in my journal. The Lord said, "Why not number the pages so you can find stuff easier." I had never ever thought of that before, and wow, it worked. The Lord only wants the best for us.

On July 1, I received another message from the Lord. I wrote, "I am sending you to Cheyenne Wells first to prove that when I say the days will be like in Noah's time, I am saying that even the people you know will be skeptical about what you are telling them. Stay strong, and finish the race I have put you in. The race will be finished when we meet eye!"

This was the message that began to make me understand somewhat where the Lord was going with me. In July, I visited many churches in the area and shared what the Lord was doing in my life. I drove over to CW and visited with a lady who, with her husband, owns a hardware store. I had never ever talked with her about God before. I asked her who the minister was at the church they attended. She told me that they were looking for a minister. We visited for a while, and I shared what the Lord was doing in my life. She listened and invited me to come to their church. I went Sunday and shared to many that I've known for many years what the Lord had been doing. They listened and asked me to come back. I will be totally honest, I was scared. I had never done anything like that before. I was not the person who went to social events often, and I wasn't even going to church at this time.

On July 3, the Lord said,

> For I know the thoughts that I think toward you says the Lord, thoughts of peace, and not of evil, to give you a future and a hope. Then you will call upon Me and go and pray to Me, and I will listen to you, and you will seek Me and find Me when you search for Me with all your heart. (Jeremiah 29:11–13)

> For He Himself has said, "I will never leave you nor forsake you." (Hebrews 13:5)

On July 4, I woke up like I had been for many months now, writing out the Word. That day, I heard a sermon on keeping the faith. I was still not knowing where the Lord was actually taking me. After I finished my writing for the day, the Lord spoke to me, saying,

> I charge you therefore before God and the Lord Jesus Christ, who will judge the living and the dead at His appearing and His Kingdom. Preach the word! Be ready in season, and out of season. Convince, rebuke, exhort, with all longsuffering and teaching. For the time will come when they will not endure sound doctrine, but according to their own desires, because then have itching ears, they will heap up for themselves teachers, and they will turn their ears away from the truth, and be turned aside to fables. But you, be watchful in all

things, endure afflictions, do the work of an evangelist, fulfill your ministry. (2 Timothy 4:1–5)

After I wrote this in my journal, I had a feeling come over me, and I was finally beginning to accept and understand what the Lord was attempting to do through me. It was like a burden lifted off me, and I moved forward. I was beginning to understand how God uses His living Word to communicate with us.

On July 6, as I was wondering in my thoughts if I was really ready for this or meant to do this, the Lord revealed to me the verse, "But the Lord said to me, 'Do not say I am a youth, for you shall go to all to whom I send you, and whatever I command you, you shall speak'" (Jer. 1:7).

And we know that all things work together for good to those who love God, to those who are the called according to His purpose. (Romans 8:28)

It is amazing how the Lord uses His means to get through to us, but we must remember that everything is in His timing, and we must "rest in the Lord, and wait patiently for Him" (Ps. 37:7 (first part of the verse)).

On July 13, the Lord revealed, "But as for you, continue in the things which you have learned and been assured of, knowing from whom you have learned them" (2 Tim. 3:14).

In all your ways acknowledge Him, and He shall direct your paths. (Proverbs 3:6)

As the days went on, the Lord was revealing many things that I have written in my journal, concerning current events and Scripture that was written many years ago that are now today coming to pass.

He also told me, "If you do not keep your mind and heart focused on Me, then you will begin to sink like Peter did. I am the Way and the Truth. Always trust Me!"

I will give you a new heart and put a new Spirit within you. I will take the heart of stone out of your flesh. I will put My Spirit within you and cause you to walk in My Statutes. (Ezekiel 36:26–27)

This Book of the Law shall not depart from your mouth, but you shall meditate in it day and night, that you may observe to do according to all that is written in it. For then you shall make your way prosperous, and then you will have good success. (Joshua 1:8)

On July 17, I was watching a sermon on Samson. It was a very good teaching, and after I heard it, I understood how God dealt with him.

After it was over, the Lord revealed to me: "The reason America is in trouble is that it has removed Me (God) from everything. America was founded on Biblical principles. Just like when I (God) removed My Spirit from Samson, America is without My Spirit now as well." Wow, it was all starting to make sense. We are in trouble! Then the Lord revealed this verse to me: "So the Lord said to him, who has made man's mouth? Or who makes the mute, the deaf, the seeing, or the blind? Have not I, the Lord? Now therefore go, and I will be with your mouth and teach you what you shall say" (Exod. 4:11–12).

"Have I not commanded you? Be strong and of good courage, do not be afraid, nor be dismayed, for the Lord your God is with you wherever you go." (Joshua 1:9)

The Savior wants to use your life as a platform for His power. So when He calls, don't worry about whether you're smart enough, talented, or beautiful enough. Just obey Him wholeheartedly, and He will surely magnify Himself through you. This is a quote from

Charles Stanley. The Lord uses him and others throughout this journey to speak to me.

> Blessed is the man whom You instruct, O Lord,
> and teach out of Your law. (Psalm 94:12)

> Let me know Your ways that I may know You,
> so that I may find favor in Your sight. (Exodus
> 33:13)

Most of the instructions I got came while I was sitting at the table and doing my daily writing. I would be writing, then a thought would enter my mind, and I would go to my journal and write what the Holy Spirit put on my mind at that time. On July 18, I got this thought: "The Lord uses the story of Noah as a preview of the future rapture. First of all, Noah had faith. He built an ark, and when all allowed to enter had entered, the Lord raised them up above the water. One day, soon we who believe will be called up to meet the Lord in the air."

Then the Lord revealed this verse to me: "But blessed are your eyes for they see, and your ears for they hear, for assuredly, I say to you that many prophets and righteous men desire to see what you see, and did not see it, and to hear what you hear, and did not hear it" (Matt. 13:16–17).

> If any of you lacks wisdom, let him ask of God
> who gives to all liberally and without reproach,
> and it will be given to him. (James 1:5)

> Now He who has prepared us for this very thing
> is God, who also has given us the Spirit as a guar-
> antee. (2 Corinthians 5:5)

As the days went on, the Lord was slowly revealing to me where this journey was going, and He revealed a sermon to me in Luke 16:19–31. On the twenty-fourth of July, this was what I wrote: "This is Jesus's example of where people who are not saved go when they die, awaiting the judgment. Believers and nonbelievers are separated by a great chasm between the two." When I heard the sermon that explains the parable of the rich man and Lazarus, I was blown away. I had never ever heard it taught that way. As I wrote in my message to the youth, I was fifty-seven years old when I heard the truth about where a person's soul goes when they die. No one ever told me that I would spend eternity with a new body. I now know the truth, and I am thankful for the Lord revealing to me that: "The Lord is not slack concerning His promise, as some count slackness, but is longsuffering toward us, not willing that any should perish, but that all should come to repentance" (2 Pet. 3:9).

Then on July 31, the Lord revealed the parable of the ten virgins. I wrote in my journal on that day: "The parable of the ten virgins is an example of how many will be left behind. Jesus said, 'Depart from Me, I never knew you!' These words are words no man or woman will ever want to hear. Half of the virgins were fully equipped, and the other five were just weekend warriors. We must be ready now and prepared because we don't know when the Lord will say, 'Come up here.'"

> Not everyone who says to Me, "Lord, Lord", shall enter the Kingdom of heaven, but he who does the will of My Father in heaven. Many will say to Me in that day, "Lord, Lord, have we not prophesied in Your name, cast out demons in Your name, and done many wonders in Your name?" And then I will declare to them, "I never knew you, depart from Me, you who practice lawlessness!" (Matthew 7:21–23)

After I received the two parables, on August 11, the Lord revealed my next message: "You are now prepared to go out and spread the Good News. I have prepared you to plant the seeds in as many people as possible. I gave you the last two parables to convince people where they will spend eternity apart from Me! Feed My sheep!"

And do this, knowing the time, that now it is high time to awake out of sleep, for now our salvation is nearer than when we first believed. (Romans 13:11)

On August 17, the Lord revealed to me: "I have been preparing you over the past months just like I prepared Mary to give birth to My Son, Jesus Christ. It is a process that takes time. Stay strong. Keep the faith, and the reward will be worth it, which is eternal life!"

On August 28, I gave my first-ever message in front of a congregation. All the times before when I would visit with various people after the service was over.

The week leading up to the twenty-eighth, I was having a hard time, and the enemy was really messing with my confidence. The Lord revealed the following verses to me to reassure me:

Do not worry beforehand or premeditate what you will speak. But whatever is given you in that hour, speak that, for it is not you who speaks, but the Holy Spirit. (Mark 13:11)

It is the Lord Christ you are serving. And whatever you do, do it heartily, as to the Lord and not to men, knowing that from the Lord, you will receive the reward of the inheritance, for you serve the Lord Christ. (Colossians 3:23–24)

It is so awesome to have a relationship with the Lord where He reveals things just at the right moment. The morning of my message, I was still pondering how to announce why I was giving the message. David Jeremiah did a sermon on being a "witness." The Lord gave me my answer through his message.

That morning was going as usual; I was all ready to get in my vehicle. I looked out, and my rear tire is flat. That was the first attempt by the enemy to stop me. Then my mom, who was going with me, called me and said she needed to go to the emergency room—second attempt from the enemy. We talked on the phone, and I told her I was giving my message no matter what. I took her to the hospital. I went and gave my message and picked her up after the service. On the way home, the Lord told me that I needed to tell my mom what she had missed hearing earlier at church. I just laid it out in the open and told her about the parable of the rich man and Lazarus. She had not yet received the Lord in her heart. I told her that if we were to have an accident and we both were killed, I have the comfort of knowing I will be safe in Abraham's bosom with the Lord forever. Now for her, I told her that without being "saved," she would go to another place, where there is gnawing and gnashing of teeth and eternal separation from the Lord.

> The Lord shall preserve your going out and your coming in from this time forth, and even forevermore. (Psalm 121:8)

> Those who trust in the Lord are like Mount Zion, which cannot be moved, but abides forever. As the mountains surround Jerusalem, so the Lord surrounds His people from this time forth and forever. (Psalm 125:1–2)

As the days passed, I was continuing my daily writing; now it is September. As time went on, the Lord was revealing more and more every day, especially how things are happening in the world.

> Therefore let us not sleep as others do, but let us watch and be sober. (1 Thessalonians 5:6)

On September 8, I wrote,

> Now it shall come to pass, if you diligently obey the voice of the Lord your God, to observe carefully all His commandments which I command, you today, that the Lord your God will set you

high above all nations of the earth. And all these
blessings shall come upon you and overtake you,
because you obey the voice of the Lord your God.
(Deuteronomy 6:2)

I have a pamphlet above my microwave that I am able to read
every day. It is a quote from Charles Stanley saying, *"Listening to God
is essential to walking with God."* The Lord never lets me forget that. I
can honestly say that since I have totally let God take control of my
life, that saying is very valuable to me.

The peace of God, which surpasses all understanding, will guard your hearts and minds through
Christ Jesus. (Philippians 4:7)

Therefore we also pray always for you that our
God would count you worthy of this calling, and
fulfill all the good pleasure of His goodness and
the work of faith with power, that the name of our
Lord Jesus Christ may be glorified in you, and you
in Him, according to the grace of our God and the
Lord Jesus Christ. (2 Thessalonians 1:11–12)

The Lord had me write, "I will give you the treasures of darkness and hidden riches of secret places, that you may know that I the
Lord, who calls you by name, am the God of Israel" (Isa. 45:3).

After these verses, I did not hear from the Lord for a few days,
almost a month. During this time, I was gaining insight more and
more on what is happening in the world. There is so much happening, and the sad thing for us is that the news won't report on things.
We are experiencing the events of the last days occurring before our
eyes. These will be discussed further later on.

On October 2, the Lord revealed to me: "The turning point
will be when the rapture occurs! Then all things will begin to make
sense!"

> And let us not grow weary while doing good,
> for in due season, we will reap if we do not lose
> heart. (Galatians 6:9)

As the days passed, I kept hearing the word *diligently* talked about a lot. I never knew the true meaning of the word until Sept. 23. That day, I listened to a message on the word *diligently*. It was explained that it means to want to seek the Lord with all joy and gladness. I wrote,

> But without Faith it is impossible to please Him,
> for he who comes to God must believe that he is,
> and that He is a rewarder of those who diligently
> seek Him. (Hebrews 11:6)

> So then faith cometh by hearing; and hearing by
> the Word of God. (Romans 10:17)

> In all your ways acknowledge Him, and He shall
> direct your paths. (Proverbs 3:6)

> And you shall know the truth, and the truth shall
> make you free. (John 8:32)

On October 17, the Lord revealed to me: "Remember how I used Paul, who was persecuting My people, to become a man who changed many lives. I am using you the same way. You don't need a degree in anything. Just always listen to My voice!"

> God is faithful, by whom you were called unto
> the fellowship of His Son, Jesus Christ our Lord.
> (1 Corinthians 1:9)

> For I am not ashamed of the gospel of Christ,
> for it is the power of God to Salvation for every-
> one who believes, to the Jews first and also for

the Greek. For in it the righteousness of God is revealed from faith to faith, as it is written: "The just shall live by faith." (Romans 1:16–17)

As I was doing my daily writing throughout October, there were many times I would have thoughts of my journal becoming a book. I had never had those before. Then the Lord showed me videos of people who have given their testimonies, saying how the Lord had moved them to write a book. This is exactly how it started with me. In my first message, I told the congregation, "Me standing up there in front of them and giving this message, I would have never ever thought it to be possible." On October 23, the Lord had me write: "Moses met Me on Mount Sinai to receive My Word and laws. Paul went to Arabia for three years to learn My Word. I am using your kitchen table as Mount Sinai to teach you My Word." In Galatians 1:11–17, Paul explains how he is taught by God, not by man. When I went back and read what I had wrote, it all was making sense. The Lord has everything on His time line. He had revealed everything from that point to me, for the exact reasoning. From that day, my journey took another turn. Now I am being prepared to write my first-ever book. The Lord is amazing; when I first started this journey, now over a year ago, I had no idea it could, and with faith, it will become a book. During the first few months, the Lord was slowly preparing me to give my first-ever message. From there, it has now become a product of what I am writing now: my first-ever book.

On November 21, I wrote from the Lord: "I am the Lord, I do not change, therefore you are not consumed, O Sons of Jacob" (Mal. 3:6).

I also got the name for the book: *From Tabletop to Mountaintop: My Journey*.

That day also, two quotes appeared on the Internet:

I don't know what today will bring, but I do know the One who knows all.

If we trust and obey, He will lead the way.

It is so awesome to see how God uses various means to speak to us.

> My sheep hear My voice, and I know them, and
> they follow Me. (John 10:27)

On December 3, the Lord told me to move forward with the book.

> No longer do I call you servants, for a servant
> does not know what his master is doing, but I
> have called you friends, for all things I have heard
> from My Father, I have made known to you.
> (John 15:15)

All those months of writing (which I still do to this day) were training days. The Lord slowly revealed so much to me over these past many months; now it's time to write my book.

On December 4, I wrote, "If a person's beliefs are not in-line with God's Word, then that person best be changing his beliefs. The Word will never change or fail to exist!"

> Have I therefore become your enemy because I
> tell you the truth? (Galatians 4:16)

On December 7 after I had finished my writing, the Lord had me write: "Be careful when you go out and speak. Many today will judge your words. Remember what My Word says, that in the last days, many will be deceived and won't want to hear the truth! Stay strong, and keep the faith. I am coming quickly!"

> Be careful how you walk, not as unwise men, but
> as wise, making the most of your time. Therefore
> do not be unwise, but understand what the will
> of the Lord is. (Ephesians 5:15–17)

Go, stand in the temple and speak to the people
all the words of this life. (Acts 5:20)

On December 8, I wrote from the Lord: "I am not looking for great and impressive people. I am seeking the weak, humble servants who put My Son first, so that they may gain strength and wisdom."

Now when they saw the boldness of Peter and
John, and perceived that they were uneducated
and untrained men, they marveled. And they
realized that they had been with Jesus. (Acts 4:13)

That verse explains my journey. When I started, I only knew the basics; I am uneducated and untrained by man as well. The Lord has been my teacher and instructor now and forevermore. As I have been on this journey, I had no idea that the Lord would change me so much or have me write this book!

Get Prepared, Not Scared!

I am using you to accomplish My plan. Many people won't go to church because they are ashamed of their lifestyle. I need you to speak to them as a friend, not a minister. People will understand when they hear it in their own understanding.

I will instruct thee and teach thee in the way which thou shalt go. I will guide thee with Mine eye. (Psalm 32:8)

On the eighteenth of June, I wrote those words and verse that the Lord revealed to me. This was the beginning of my first assignment. By this time, I had been writing the Word daily, for many months now, and as time had gone on, I was beginning to get hints from the Lord about giving a message. As I wrote earlier, I was going to the local churches, four in total in Cheyenne Wells. I started at the Christian church first. The Lord told me to start there because it was the church that I got rebaptized in. I got rebaptized because when I learned the truth about baptism, I wanted to do it right. It takes me to the verse where Jesus Himself said, "And you shall know the truth, and the truth shall make you free" (John 8:32).

Amen, amen! It's like how this whole journey has been; when I came to the understanding of the truth, it was like the scales were removed from my eyes. I now can comprehend what is going on and why.

> The Lord will guide you continually, and satisfy
> your soul in drought, and strengthen your bones.
> You shall be like a watered garden, and like a spring
> of water, whose waters do not fail. (Isaiah 58:11)

> Then your light shall break forth like the morn-
> ing, your healing shall spring forth speedily, and
> your righteousness shall go before you. The glory
> of the Lord shall be your rear guard. (Isaiah 58:8)

As I was going back through the many pages I had already written in my journal, I was seeing a setup begin just like when the Lord
revealed His letter to me. I was taking random verses this time from
the whole Bible, and when I read them back, they were becoming a
story and my instruction book for writing my messages as well as this
book.

My first hint of giving a message came after I had a conversa-
tion with my stepdad's granddaughter. I asked her if she believed in
God. She looked at me and asked me which one. She said that on the
Internet, it's saying there is more than one. It caught me off guard.
After a few seconds of talking, I tried to explain what I knew at the
time to her about God, but I could tell she was skeptical.

After her visit is when the Lord told me to concentrate on the
younger generation. Deception is the culprit, and the Internet and
social media are full of deception.

> And Jesus answered, and said to them. Take heed
> that no one deceives you. For many will come
> in My name, saying, "I am the Christ", and will
> deceive many. (Matthew 24:4–5)

As the days went on, I continued my daily writing, and on June
6, the Lord revealed the name of my first message. I called it "Get
Prepared, Not Scared." As I have written earlier, I was attending the
local churches and sharing what the Lord was doing. This went on
until August 28, when my time had come to give my message.

> Do not fear, for I am with you, do not anxiously look about you for I am your God. I will strengthen you, surely I will help you, surely I will uphold you with My righteous right hand. (Isaiah 41:10)

> The Lord is the One who goes ahead of you, He will be with you. He will not fail you or forsake you. Do not fear or be dismayed. (Deuteronomy 31:8)

My first-ever message was a brief testimony of what the Lord had been doing in my life. I had the letter from God in the pamphlet and Charles Stanley's quote on the other side of it. I explained the letter and then how the Lord stopped my drinking. I used the verse "Who has heard such a thing? Who has seen such things? Shall the earth be made to give birth in one day? Or shall a nation be born at once? For as soon as Zion travailed, she gave birth to her children" (Isa. 66:8) to begin my message.

I began with that verse because I myself was still not sure where this was all going. The Lord told me to use this verse to help explain that all things are possible with God. "I will guide you with My eye" (Ps. 32:8).

I was on a limited time and had never done that before, so I went through the steps the Lord had set for me. I explained the instructions I had received and how the Lord had been preparing me for that message.

I had so much I wanted to say, but I didn't have enough time, so the Lord laid out exactly what He wanted me to say that day.

On June 15, the Lord had me write: "Since this year I have converted to teaching you how to feed My sheep, I want you to go out and warn as many as you can while I can still be found!" That was one of the first hints for my message. I have the quote from Charles Stanley: "*Listening to God is essential to walking with God,*" and as time has gone on, I now know that it is very important to listen and, most of all, wait on the Lord. Therefore, the best way to know His voice is to get to know Him. Spend time in His Word, the Bible, and in time, you will be able to know the Lord's intentions for you.

> Therefore comfort one another with the words.
> (1 Thessalonians 4:18)

I presented a video that was revealed to me earlier in July. It is a true story of a man who was on an airplane flight when all of a sudden the pilot passed out. It is an amazing video that shows how we must be willing to listen.

> The sheep follow He because they know His
> voice. (John 10:4)

"Father God, I thank You for Your Word, and the guidance it gives me. Impress it on my heart so that I may be able to discern Your voice from all others." I don't know who wrote that quote, but it is so powerful and true.

Then the Lord reminded me with this verse: "Trust in the Lord with all your heart, and lean not on your own understanding, in all your ways acknowledge Him, and He shall direct your paths" (Prov. 3:6).

As I was sitting at my table all those days, the Lord was revealing many new things to me. When I first started my journal, one of the first verses I put in it was from Daniel. The Lord tells Daniel to seal up the book until the end.

> But you, Daniel, shut up the words, and seal the
> book until the time of the end, many shall run
> to and fro, and knowledge shall increase. (Daniel
> 12:4)

> Many shall be purified, made white, and refined,
> but the wicked shall do wickedly, and none of
> the wicked shall understand, but the wise shall
> understand. (Daniel 12:10)

I had no idea at the time that those two verses would be so true. In my first message, the Lord had me concentrate on telling my story and how I had got to that point in my walk.

The Lord had me concentrate on three issues that He had revealed to me through various sources.

> And the Lord spoke to Moses, saying, "Speak
> to the children of Israel, and say to them: 'The
> Feasts of the Lord which you shall proclaim to
> be holy convocations, these are My feasts.'"
> (Leviticus 23:12)

I had heard of some of the feasts throughout my lifetime but never knew the truth about them. It is amazing how God used these, and will again soon, to show the Jewish people that He is still in control.

There are seven in total that the Jewish people celebrate every year: four in the spring and three in the fall.

1. Feast of Passover: Jesus was crucified on Passover.
2. Feast of Unleavened Bread: It starts the day after Passover. The Jews cannot eat regular bread for seven days to remove their sin. Jesus was buried and removed all sin from the world forever.
3. Feast of Firstfruits: Jesus was resurrected on the third day, the Feast of Firstfruits.

> But now Christ is risen from the dead, and has
> become the firstfruits of those who have fallen
> asleep." (1 Corinthians 15:20)

4. Feast of Pentecost: Fifty days after Jesus left the earth, the promise of the Holy Spirit descended upon them in the upper room.

> Now when the Day of Pentecost had fully come,
> they were all with one accord in one place. And

suddenly there came a sound from heaven, as of a
rushing mighty wind, and it filled the whole house
where they were sitting. Then there appeared to
them divided tongues, as of fire, and one sat upon
each of them. And they were all filled with the
Holy Spirit and began to speak with other tongues,
as the Spirit gave them utterance. (Acts 2:1–4)

5. Feast of Trumpets: The Jews call this festival *the day of the
    unknown* and *the day of the awakening blast.*
6. Feast of Atonement: It comes ten days after the Feast of
    Trumpets. It is the holiest day in Israel for cleansing.
7. Feast of Tabernacles: Five days after the Feast of Atonement,
    for seven days, the Jews lived in booths (tents). This rep-
    resents eternity with God. These are the festivals appointed
    by God to the Jewish people forever. I had never been told
    how, when Jesus was here on this earth, He fulfilled the
    first three to the exact date. Some Bible scholars claim He
    fulfilled them even to the hour. Jesus was crucified on the
    Feast of Passover, was buried on the Feast of Unleavened
    Bread, and then rose on the Feast of Firstfruits, three days
    later. Then fifty days later, the promise was fulfilled when
    the Holy Spirit descended from heaven and the chosen
    men of God received It. The one that really caught my
    attention and the Lord had me concentrate on the most is
    the Feast of Trumpets. In Jewish tradition, on that festival,
    a trumpet is blown one hundred times in total. On the one
    hundredth time, they call it the *Last Trump.* Paul tells us
    that we will all be changed in time at the Last Trump.

Behold, I tell you a mystery. We shall not all
sleep, but we shall all be changed, in a moment,
in the twinkling of an eye, at the last trumpet.
For the trumpet will sound, and the dead will be
raised incorruptible, and we shall be changed. (1
Corinthians 15:51–52)

> For the Lord Himself will descend from heaven
> with a shout, with the voice of an archangel, and
> with the trumpet of God, and the dead in Christ
> will rise first. (1 Thessalonians 4:16)

> Now when He had spoken these things, while
> they watched, He was taken up, and a cloud
> received Him out of their sight. (Acts 1:9)

> God has gone up with a shout, the Lord with the
> sound of a trumpet. (Psalm 47:5)

To me, these verses very clearly explain the trumpet and our future! We do have to remember that Jesus Himself said:

> But of that day and hour no one knows, no, not
> even the angels of heaven, but My Father only.
> (Matthew 24:36)

I learned so much about the festivals, and the Lord reminded me that He is in control and everything happens on His time line. So fear not!

While I was preparing my first written message, it was wheat harvest time, and over the earlier months, the Lord was telling me to get out and plant the seed. On May 21, the Lord revealed to me: "Don't get upset. You can't make anyone believe. Remember it is as in the days of Noah. People won't believe, but don't give up. Just plant the seed!"

On the eleventh of August, I wrote from the Lord: "You are now prepared to go out and spread the Good News. I have prepared you to plant the seed in as many people as possible. I gave you the last two parables to try to convince people where they will spend eternity apart from Me! Feed My sheep!" Then on the nineteenth of August, I wrote: "When I tell you to plant the seed, I am saying that you are like a farmer. He plants the seed, and I provide everything to make it grow. Keep the faith, and I will provide the harvest!"

> So shall My word be that goes forth from My mouth, it shall not return to Me void, but it shall accomplish what I please, and it shall prosper in the thing for which I sent it. (Isaiah 55:11)

Then I moved on to the two parables that the Lord had me concentrate on for the message. The first was the parable of the ten virgins. Earlier in the week, I heard a sermon on that parable, and it was explained like I had never heard it explained before. I had read that parable in the past, but when I really read it, I came to an understanding of it.

It all made sense. The pastor took the two-thousand-year-old parable and brought it to the modern day. He explained how so many people today will attend church on Sunday and then return to their everyday lives when they leave. Many live their lives as a weekend warrior: one day of service then six days of worldly lusts. He used an example of ten people who were attending church, and five of them remembered they forgot their Bibles in their vehicles. So while they were out getting them, the teacher came to get the class. When they returned, the others were gone, and the door was shut.

> Not everyone who says to Me, "Lord, Lord," shall enter the Kingdom of heaven, but he who does the will of My Father in heaven. Many will say to Me in that day, "Lord, Lord, have we not prophesied in Your name, cast out demons in Your name, and done many wonders in Your name?" And then I will declare to them, I never knew you, depart from Me, you who practice lawlessness! (Matthew 7:21–23)

Wow, this was a wake-up call. I was one of those same people, who back in my past, when I was attending church, I would leave and start drinking later that day.

The way the pastor explained the parable was so true. Many today go to church only to look good in the community.

> Blessed is the man whom You instruct, O Lord,
> and teach out of Your Law. (Psalm 94:12)

> And do not be conformed to this world, but be
> transformed by the renewing of your mind, that
> you may prove what is that good and acceptable
> and perfect will of God. (Romans 12:2)

I am so blessed that the Lord has revealed the truth to me. I was thinking that because I was going to church, then going back to the world views, everything was okay. Wow, I was wrong. When Jesus Himself said, "Depart from Me. I never knew you," I told the congregation that day that those are the words no man or woman will ever want to hear. I myself was in that category, and I know many, just around my area, who are doing the same. The Lord has taught me,

> Remember the former things of old, for I am
> God, and there is no other. I am God, and there
> is none like Me. Declaring the End from the
> Beginning, and from ancient times things that
> are not yet done, saying, "My counsel shall stand,
> and I will do My pleasure." (Isaiah 46:9–10)

> This Book of the Law shall not depart from your
> mouth but you shall meditate in it day and night
> that you may observe to do according to all that
> is written in it. For then you will make your way
> prosperous, and then you will have good success.
> (Joshua 1:8)

As I have been writing the Word every day, I can honestly say that the Lord has blessed me with so much knowledge and understanding of His Word. Thank You, Father.

I then moved on to the next parable, which is the parable of Lazarus and the rich man. Now as the months had gone by, I would talk to Mom and Larry, my stepdad, and try to explain what was coming and what would happen if they did not get saved. On the week of my upcoming message, I heard a sermon on Lazarus and the rich man. A lot of what I was sharing was what I had known as well. I heard the parable of Lazarus and the rich man and how Jesus explained where a person's spirit goes after they die. We, as believers, call this falling asleep. I was fifty-seven years old before I knew and understood any of this.

Jesus Himself said in Luke, chapter 16:19–31:

> There was a certain rich man who was clothed in purple and fine linen and fared sumptuously every day. But there was a certain beggar named Lazarus, full of sores, who was laid at his gate, desiring to be fed with the crumbs which fell from the rich man's table. Moreover the dogs came and licked his sores. So it was that the beggar died, and was carried by the angels to Abraham's bosom. The rich man also died and was buried. And being in torments in Hades, he lifted up his eyes and saw Abraham afar off, and Lazarus in his bosom. Then he cried out and said, "Father Abraham, have mercy on me, and send Lazarus that he may dip the tip of his finger in water and cool my tongue, for I am tormented in this flame." But Abraham said, "Son, remember that in your lifetime you received your good things, and likewise Lazarus evil things, but now he is comforted and you are tormented. And besides all this, between us and you there is a great gulf fixed, so that those who want to pass from here to you cannot, nor can those from there pass to us." Then he said, "I beg you therefore father, that you would send him to my father's house, for I have five brothers, that he may testify to them, lest they also come to this place of torment." Abraham said to him. "They have Moses and the

prophets, let them hear them." And he said, "No, father Abraham, but if one goes to them from the dead, they will repent." But he said to him, "If they do not hear Moses and the prophets, neither will they be persuaded though one rise from the dead."

That parable explains where a person's soul will go when they die. It also explains that there is no other opportunity to accept the gospel of truth after a person dies. The Lord had me call my message "Get Prepared, Not Scared." Now I totally understand why. I told the congregation that like the Bible says, "Tomorrow is promised to no man." We must be ready now, and then we won't worry about being scared of the things that are written that will be fulfilled.

And do this, know the time, that now it is high time to awake out of sleep, for now our salvation is nearer than when we first believed. (Romans 13:11)

I finished talking about the two parables and noticed I was out of time. I finished my message with this quote that I wrote: "My mission is to 'feed My sheep!' I have been so blessed by how the Lord has shown me so much and revealed to me. I pray that this has helped as many people as possible to seek the Lord while He may still be found. One day very soon, I do believe that the opportunity will be gone forever. God bless you all! Amen, amen."

This is a faithful saying: for if we died with Him. We shall also live with Him. If we endure, we shall also reign with Him. If we deny Him, He also will deny us. If we are faithless, He remains faithful. He cannot deny Himself. (2 Timothy 2:11–13)

THE YOUTH

<hr>

Now a few days after I had given my first message in front of a congregation, I was driving myself and Larry to Burlington, Colorado. Larry had some prescriptions to pick up. This is a monthly trip we make, and the past few months, I have been using every trip we make to plant the seed to him and Mom.

> The Lord God will be with you wherever you go.
> (Joshua 1:9)

> I will guide you with My eye. (Psalm 32:8)

When we got to Burlington, I parked where we normally do, and this time as I park, right in front of me, on the building on the main street, there was a big mural on the window mentioning God. So while Larry is getting his meds, I went in to check out the building. I met a young man named *David,* and we talked for a few minutes. He told me that he was the youth leader and they were just moving into that building. I didn't have much time, and they were busy as well, so we exchanged phone numbers.

The days went on, and Mom, Larry, and I were driving back from Lamar, Colorado. That's where they are both doctors now. As I was driving, the Lord had me call David from Burlington. I called him and set up a time to meet so I could share what the Lord had been doing in my life up to that time. Over the weekend, I was reminded by the Lord that I needed to concentrate on the youth.

He took me back to when I had the conversation with Larry's grand-daughter and how the Internet was spreading deception. Today's current events are setting the world up to be deceived by one person. The media is using fake sources to mislead us, the people. This is an example of how the world will be in the last days when the antichrist comes on the scene. What's sad is that many will believe the lie.

> Call to Me, and I will answer you, and show you great and mighty things, which you do not know. (Jeremiah 33:3)

> It shall come to pass that before they call, I will answer, and while they are still speaking, I will hear. (Isaiah 65:24)

I didn't have to ask any questions; those two verses were telling me that my next message would be for the *youth*. I made it to Burlington and had a great sit-down with David. I showed him my journal and shared my "letter from God" with him. He shared the plans that the church had for the youth. We discussed setting up a time and date to hopefully give my message to the local youth in the area. At that time, I had not written my message specifically concentrating on the youth yet.

> And we know that all things work together for good to those who love God, to those who are called according to His purpose. (Romans 8:28)

> For You are my rock and my fortress, therefore, for Your name's sake, lead me and guide me. (Psalm 31:3)

So I began writing my message concentrating on the youth.

> When thou goest: thy steps shall not be hindered, and when thou runnest, thou shalt not stumble.

Take fast hold of instruction, let her not go, keep
her, for she is thy life. (Proverbs 4:12–13)

Seek ye first the Kingdom of God, and His righteousness and all these things shall be added to
you. (Matthew 6:33)

Men and women, I am here today to claim that these two verses
have become a reality for me. I am fifty-seven years old, and now I
have more peace, hope, and joy than I have ever had in my entire life.
When I finally let the Lord break me down and show me that this is
not about me, but the glory of His Son, Jesus Christ, I began to grow
in wisdom and knowledge and understanding.

Trust in the Lord with all your heart and lean
not on your own understanding, in all your ways
acknowledge Him, and He shall direct your
paths. (Proverbs 3:6)

Thy Word is a lamp unto my feet, and a light
unto my path. (Psalm 119:105)

However when He the Spirit of Truth has come,
He will guide you into all truth. (John 16:13)

It is amazing how the Lord knows exactly how to keep His chosen ones going. For me personally, since I have been on this journey,
the Lord has had me adjust so I could keep the faith and continue on
this journey. When I first started writing out the Bible many months
ago now, I was struggling. I had a hard time staying awake and concentrating. One morning, I started playing a song that had been on
my mind and that I had been listening to already. It's called "Drums
of War." That same day, there was a sermon on Jerusalem. They were
sounding the alarm, the drums of war!

This began my new approach every morning and still does to
this day. The Lord knows all, and when I was in my youth, I loved

sports. I used to listen to music loud, and it would get me motivated and full of energy. I would listen, if possible, before every game or sporting event. This is how the Lord began to teach me His way. Today I still wake up around 2:00–2:30 a.m., and from 3:00 to 4:00 a.m., I have a playlist I use every morning to get me motivated. We have to begin exercising before we can become a member of God's team. In order to be on God's team, we must believe He exists!

> He who believes in Me, as the Scripture has said, out of his heart will flow rivers of living water. (John 7:38)

> "You are My witnesses," says the Lord, "and My servant whom I have chosen, that you may know and believe Me, and understand that I am He." (Isaiah 43:10)

In order to be able to understand and believe, we must remember that *listening to God is essential to walking with God!* When we come to that understanding, we are on our way to salvation.

Most of us, while growing up, enjoyed the opportunity to compete in different sporting events. We all have that same opportunity to become a member of God's team today. I was told by someone many years ago that we are all on a personal track meet. We are a member of the church if we are believers in Him. But we all have our own talents and abilities.

> Do you not know that those who run in a race all run, but one receives the prize? Run in such a way that you may obtain it. And everyone who competes for the prize is temperate in all things. Now they do it to obtain a perishable crown, but we for an imperishable crown. (1 Corinthians 9:24–25)

Before one of the biggest sporting events in the world starts, it takes a flip of a coin to determine which team receives the ball first.

In life, we are a team when we belong to the church, but we all have to make that personal decision in our lives to accept Jesus or not.

Just like a coin, we only have two choices.

Heads: we spend eternity with Him forever.

Tails: we spend eternity separated from Him forever.

That's why we need to *get prepared, not scared* now, because "Tomorrow is promised to no man."

> Seek the Lord while He may be found, call upon Him while He is near. (Deuteronomy 28:1–2)

> When we become members of the Lord's team, we can have the peace knowing that: "The Lord is the One who goes ahead of you, He will be with you. He will not fail you or forsake you. Do not fear or be dismayed." (Deuteronomy 31:8)

Our lives are in a competition daily. We have to be trained in the Word so we can overcome every blitz or trick play the competition (the enemy) may throw at us. In the game, the opponent's objective is to defeat the other team. In life, our opponent (the enemy) wants to not only defeat us, but he also wants to destroy us.

> Likewise exhort the young men to be sober-minded, in all things showing yourself to be a pattern of good works, in doctrine showing integrity, reverence, incorruptibility, sound speech that cannot be condemned, that one who is an opponent may be ashamed, having nothing evil to say of you. (Titus 2:6–8)

When a person enters an event, they have to be suited for that event. Some sports require more equipment than others. But in order to participate, we must have our equipment on. In our game of life, in order to be able to deal with the enemy, we must use the equipment the Lord provides for us.

> Finally, my brethren, be strong in the Lord, and in
> the power of His might. Put on the whole armor
> of God, that you may be able to stand against the
> wiles of the devil. For we do not wrestle against
> flesh and blood, but against principalities, against
> powers, against the rulers of the darkness of this
> age, against spiritual hosts of wickedness in the
> heavenly places. Therefore take up the whole
> armor of God, that you may be able to withstand
> in the evil day, and having done all to stand.
> (Ephesians 6:10–13)

The Lord gives us the belt of truth to hold the breastplate of righteousness on. For our feet, He gives us the gospel of peace. We get a shield of faith, a helmet of salvation, and the sword of the Spirit, which is the Word of God. With all these, we are able to withstand all the fiery darts the enemy attacks us with and to endure any situation in life that may come upon us.

> For bodily exercise profits a little, but godliness
> is profitable for all things, having promise of the
> life that now is, and of that which is to come. (1
> Timothy 4:8)

I look back now on my life growing up, and I never knew any of the things I now know, thanks to the Lord. I went to Sunday school, church camps, and many youth groups while growing up, and no one ever explained the truth. I had no idea that when we die, we will spend eternity in one of two places. Men and women, we only have one chance to get it right, because tomorrow is promised to no man.

> Therefore we also, since we are surrounded by so
> great a cloud of witnesses, let us lay aside every
> weight, and the sin which so easily ensnares us,

and let us run with endurance, the race that is set
before us. (Hebrews 12:1)

Now is the time to accept the free gift God gives each and every
one of us, which is eternal life with Him. With that free gift comes,
peace, joy, comfort, healing, wisdom, strength, and so much more.
Jesus, Himself, tells us:

I have said these things to you, that in Me you
may have peace. In the world you will have tribulation, but take heart, I have overcome the world!
(John 16:33)

When I was growing up, we didn't have the electronic devices
that there are today. We had bikes and trucks; the girls had dolls to
play with. We had to make our own entertainment. Today, though,
is a whole different ball game. There are so many devices to choose
from. Many of these are able to connect to the Internet, and it can
be both good and bad. I will admit that some of the information I
received from the Lord was through the Internet. He has used many
different online messages to teach me and guide me through this
journey. The Internet is like a coin as well; there are two choices to
choose from: heads or tails on a coin and good information or misinformation from the Internet. With the coin toss, we can't control
which side wins. But with the Internet, we do have a choice to choose
the good or bad info.

That's where we have to be careful. The Internet is full of deception, concentrating on the young generation.

Blessed are those who hunger and thirst for righteousness, for they shall be filled. (Matthew 5:6)

The very first warning Jesus gave His disciples
was "And Jesus answered, and said to them. Take
heed that no one deceives you." (Matthew 24:4)

Deception is probably the enemy's number one weapon he uses against us. The battles we are in daily mostly start in the mind. The enemy wants us to believe the lie. His goal is to keep as many of God's children from entering the kingdom of heaven, but Jesus clearly tells us:

> To the pure, all things are pure, but to those who are defiled and unbelieving, nothing is pure, but even their mind and conscience are defiled. (Titus 1:15)

> For the Lord gives wisdom, from His mouth come knowledge and understanding. He stores up sound wisdom for the upright: He is a shield to those who walk uprightly. He guards the paths of justice, and preserves the way of His saints. (Proverbs 2:6–8)

As I was writing out my message, *The Youth*, the Lord was revealing things like He had been doing throughout this journey. The Internet kept coming up, and I wrote this from the Lord: "You, as parents, must be involved. There is much deception through the Internet, and it is focusing on the youth. You must be watchful in all their actions."

> Train up a child in the way he should go, and when he is old he will not depart from it. (Proverbs 22:6)

> But I say to you, that for every idle word men may speak, they will give account of it in the day of judgment. (Matthew 12:36)

Another way the enemy uses misinformation is through the laws. Now, here in America, it is okay to marry the same sex. We have laws that protect the gay community. Men and women, God made man and woman! There are no exceptions. The enemy is deceiving people's minds by having them believe they are not who God created them to be.

> You shall not lie with a male as with a woman. It
> is an abomination. (Leviticus 18:32)

The Lord is very clear with that verse. Now some schools are teaching our young children that it is okay to not know which sex they are. They are deceiving the young right through our school system.

> How can a young man cleanse his way? By taking
> heed to Your Word. (Psalm 119:9)

That's why parents have to be involved in their children's lives.

> Blessed is the man who walks not in the counsel
> of the ungodly, nor stands in the path of sinners,
> nor sits in the seat of the scornful, but his delight
> is in the law of the Lord, and in His law he med-
> itates day and night. (Psalm 1:1–2)

Men and women, when I began this message, I talked about our lives being in a track meet and how we need to use all equipment the Lord provides to us to protect ourselves from the enemy's tactics.

> And let us not grow weary while doing good, for
> in due season we will reap if we do not lose heart.
> (Galatians 6:9)

We must keep the faith and finish the race the Lord has put each one of us in who He has created.

> Brethren, I do not count myself to have appre-
> hended, but one thing I do, forgetting those

thing which are behind, and reaching forward to
those things which are ahead. I press toward the
goal for the prize of the upward call of God in
Christ Jesus. (Philippians 3:13–14)

In our game of life, those of us who put our faith in Jesus Christ
and endure to the end will receive many crowns: the crown of victory, the crown of exultation, the crown of life, and the crown of
righteousness.

Finally, there is laid up for me the crown of righteousness, which the Lord, the righteous Judge
will give to me on that Day, and not to me only
but also to all who have loved His appearing. (2
Timothy 4:8)

My ultimate goal for the race I am currently in is to finish the
race and cast my crowns down at Jesus's feet and hear these words:
"His Lord said to him, 'Well done, good and faithful servant, you
were faithful over a few things. I will make you ruler over many
things. Enter into the joy of the Lord'" (Matt. 25:21).

Therefore comfort one another with these words.
(1 Thessalonians 4:18)

Remember now your Creator in the days of your
youth, before the difficult days come, and the
years draw near when you say, "I have no pleasure
in them." (Ecclesiastes 12:1)

But the Lord is faithful, who will establish you,
and guard you from the evil one. (2 Thessalonians
3:3)

So men and women, hear the words of Jesus Himself:

> He who believes and is baptized will be saved,
> but he who does not believe, will be condemned.
> (Mark 16:16)

That finished my written message from the Lord to *the youth.*

The Good News

As the days moved on and as I was continuing my daily writing, the Lord was having me go back through my journal and begin a new written message. He wanted me to concentrate on all the verses I had at the time that pertained to all the wonderful promises He gives us through His Word. To be honest, I was amazed at how many He had revealed to me: some I had heard before but many I had never heard.

This message came to me just like my "letter from God" did. This time it was myself who went back through my journal, and the Holy Spirit is the One who has put them in sequence. What is so amazing to me is that the verses contained in this message have been revealed to me over an eleven-month time frame (and still being revealed as I write this book).

I do not know what today will bring, but I do know the One who knows all! If we trust and obey, He will lead the way.

> And he who does not take his cross and follow
> after Me, is not worthy of Me. (Matthew 10:38)
>
> So then faith cometh by hearing, and hearing by
> the Word of God. (Romans 10:17)

We must remember that Christianity is not a religion: it is a personal relationship with Jesus Christ.

For we walk by faith, not by sight. (2 Corinthians 5:7)

By faith Noah, being divinely warned of things not yet seen, moved with Godly fear, prepared an ark for the saving of his household, by which he condemned the world and became heir of the righteous, which is according to faith. (Hebrews 11:7)

Remember the former things of old, for I am God, and there is no other. I am God, and there is none like Me. Declaring the end from the beginning, and from ancient times things that are not yet done, saying, "My counsel shall stand, and I will do all My pleasure." (Isaiah 46:9–10)

I say then, Walk in the Spirit, and you shall not fulfill the lust of the flesh. (Galatians 5:16)

There is therefore now no condemnation to those who are in Christ Jesus who do not walk according to the flesh, but according to the Spirit. (Romans 8:1)

I, even I, have spoken, yes, I have called him, I have brought him, and his way will prosper. (Isaiah 48:15)

The Lord your God will be with you wherever you go. (Joshua 1:9)

"You are My witnesses," says the Lord, "and My servant whom I have chosen, that you may know and believe Me, and understand that I am He." (Isaiah 43:10)

God has chosen the foolish things of the world to put to shame the wise, and God has chosen the weak things of the world to put to shame the things which are mighty. (1 Corinthians 1:27)

If you love Me, keep My commandments. And I will pray the Father, and He will give you another Helper, that He may abide with you forever, even the Spirit of truth, whom the world cannot receive, because it neither sees Him nor knows Him, but you know Him, for He dwells with you and will be in you. (John 14:15–17)

God, who made the world and everything in it, since He is Lord of heaven, and earth, does not dwell in temples made with hands. Nor is He worshiped with men's hands, as though He needed anything, since He gives to all life, breath, and all things. And He has made from one blood every nation of men to dwell on all the face of the earth, and has determined their preappointed times and the boundaries of their habitation, so that they should seek the Lord, in the hope that they might grope for Him and find Him, though He is not far from each one of us, for in Him we live and move and have our being, as also some of your own poets have said, "For we are also His offspring." Therefore, since we are the offspring of God, we ought not to think that the Divine Nature is like gold or silver or stone, something shaped by art and man's devising. Truly, these things of ignorance God overlooked, but now commands all men everywhere to repent, because He has appointed a day on which He will judge the world in righteousness by the Man whom He has ordained. He has given assurance of this to all by raising Him from the dead. (Acts 17:24–31)

Let us therefore come boldly to the throne of grace, that we may obtain mercy and find grace to help in time of need. (Hebrews 4:16)

To him who overcomes I will grant to sit with Me on My throne, as I also overcame and sat down with My Father on His throne. (Revelation 3:21)

If any of you lacks wisdom, let him ask of God, who gives to all liberally and without reproach, and it will be given to him. (James 1:5)

As for God, His way is perfect, the word of the Lord is proven, He is a shield to all who trust in Him. (Psalm 18:30)

Consecrate yourselves therefore, and be holy, for I am the Lord your God. (Leviticus 20:7)

Assuredly, I say to you, this generation will by no means pass away till all things are fulfilled. (Luke 21:32)

Watch therefore, and pray always that you may be counted worthy to escape all these things that will come to pass, and to stand before the Son of Man. (Luke 21:36)

Behold, the former things have come to pass, and new things I declare, before they spring forth, I tell you of them. (Isaiah 42:9)

Surely the Lord God does nothing unless He reveals His secrets to His servants, the prophets. (Amos 3:7)

So then faith cometh by hearing, and hearing by the Word of God. (Romans 10:17)

Call to Me, and I will answer you, and show you great and mighty things which you do not know. (Jeremiah 33:3)

It shall come to pass that before they call, I will answer, and while they are still speaking, I will hear. (Isaiah 65:24)

For the Day of the Lord upon all nations is near, as you have done, it shall be done to you your reprisal shall return upon your own head. (Obadiah 1:15)

"You are My witnesses," says the Lord, "and My servant whom I have chosen, that you may know and believe Me, and understand that I am He. (Isaiah 43:10)

Therefore comfort one another with these words. (1 Thessalonians 4:18)

Now, brethren, concerning the coming of our Lord Jesus Christ and our gathering together to Him, we ask you not to be soon shaken in mind or troubled, either by Spirit or by word, or by letter, as if from us, as though the day of Christ had come. Let no one deceive you by any means, for that Day will not come unless the falling away comes first, and the man of sin is revealed, the son of perdition. (2 Thessalonians 2:1–3)

For God did not appoint us to wrath, but to obtain salvation through our Lord Jesus Christ. (1 Thessalonians 5:9)

And to wait for His Son from heaven, whom He raised from the dead, even Jesus who delivers us from the wrath to come. (Thessalonians 1:10)

In My father's house are many mansions, if it were not so, I would have told you. I go to prepare a place for you. And if I go and prepare a place for you. I will come again and receive you to Myself, that where I am, there you may be also. And where I go you know, and the way you know. (John 14:2–4)

You therefore, beloved, knowing this beforehand, be on your guard, so that you are not carried away by the error of unprincipled men and fall from your own steadfastness. (2 Peter 3:17)

Forgetting those things which are behind, and reaching forward to those things which are ahead, I press toward the goal for the prize of the upward call of God in Christ Jesus. (Philippians 3:13–14)

For whatever things were written before were written for our learning, that we through the patience and comfort of the Scriptures might have hope. (Romans 15:4)

Alas! For that Day is great, so that none is like it, and it is the time of Jacob's trouble, but he shall be saved out of it. (Jeremiah 30:7)

Behold, I tell you a mystery. We shall not all sleep, but we shall all be changed, in a moment, in the twinkling of an eye, at the last trumpet. For the trumpet will sound and the dead will be raised incorruptible, and we shall be changed. (1 Corinthians 15:51–52)

For the Lord Himself will descend from heaven with a shout, with the voice of an archangel, and with the trumpet of God, and the dead in Christ will rise first. (1 Thessalonians 4:16)

Now when He had spoken these things, while they watched. He was taken up, and a cloud received Him out of their sight. (Acts 1:9)

God has gone up with a shout, the Lord with the sound of a trumpet. (Psalm 47:5)

After these things I looked, and behold, a door standing open in heaven. And the first voice which I heard was like a trumpet speaking with me, saying, "Come up here, and I will show you things which must take place after this." (Revelation 4:1)

You, also be patient: Establish your hearts, for the coming of the Lord is at hand. (James 5:8)

The Lord is the One who goes ahead of you, He will be with you, He will not fail you or forsake you. Do not fear or be dismayed. (Deuteronomy 31:8)

Now may the God of hope fill you with all joy and peace in believing that you may abound in hope by the power of the Holy Spirit. (Romans 15:13)

Then the Lord came down upon Mount Sinai, on the top of the mountain. And the Lord called Moses to the top of the mountain, and Moses went up. (Exodus 19:2)

Do not fear, nor be afraid, have I not told you from that time, and declared it? You are My witnesses, is there of God besides Me? Indeed, there is no other Rock, I know not One. (Isaiah 44:8)

But sanctify the Lord God in your hearts, and always be ready to give a defense to everyone who asks you a reason for the hope that is in you, with meekness and fear. (1 Peter 3:15)

Draw near to God, and He will draw near to you. Cleanse your hands, you sinners, and purify your hearts, you double-minded. (James 4:8)

Blessed is the man whom You instruct, O Lord, and teach out of Your law. (Psalm 94:12)

For He Himself has said, "I will never leave you nor forsake you." (Hebrews 13:5)

Hypocrites! You can discern the face of the sky and of the earth, but how is it you do not discern this time? (Luke 12:56)

Those who are led by the Spirit of God are the children of God. (Romans 8:14)

Call upon Me in the day of trouble, I will deliver you, and you shall glorify Me. (Psalm 50:15)

Whoever is wise will observe these things, and they will understand the lovingkindness of the Lord. (Psalm 107:43)

So, you, likewise, when you see these things happening, know that the Kingdom of God is near. (Luke 21:20)

Lead me in Your truth, and teach me, for You are the God of my Salvation. On You I wait all the day. (Psalm 25:5)

But the end of all things is at hand; therefore, be serious and watchful in your prayers. (1 Peter 4:7)

Behold, I am with you and will keep you wherever you go, and will bring you back to this land, for I will not leave you until I have done what I have spoken to you. (Genesis 28:15)

Therefore, as the elect of God, holy and beloved, put on tender mercies, kindness, humility, meekness, longsuffering, bearing with one another, and forgiving one another, if anyone has a complaint against another, even as Christ forgave you. So you also must do. But above all these things put on love, which is the bond of perfection. And let the peace of God rule in your hearts, to which also you were called in one body, and be thankful. (Colossians 3:12–15)

Those were the verses the Lord had me take from my journal.

Dear God, thank You for sharing Your wisdom and knowledge with me. Help me to boldly share Your Word and Your never-ending love with those around me today and every day.

Amen, amen.

INSPIRING WORDS

When this journey first began, now over a year ago, the Lord had me start with listening to David Jeremiah on television. As I would do my daily writing, when the TV shows were over, I would go to YouTube and watch the world news and other sermons by various teachers. I have probably watched hundreds of hours of sermons and videos over the past year. As I would be watching and listening, the Lord would have me write certain quotes, and He also revealed quotes for me to use from many various books I have as well.

Throughout this whole journey, the Lord has never ever ceased to amaze me. Just like He had me write: "When we fully understand Him, we don't have to search the Scriptures. They will find us." Wow, what an amazingly true statement.

This section in my journey concentrates on three pastors I have listened to many times over the years. They are awesome teachers that tell the truth! The Lord has taught me so much through these men, and I want to share the quotes the Lord had me write over the past months. They are from Charles Stanley, David Jeremiah, and John Hagee and a few frow unknown authors. I pray that they help anyone who reads them. When I went back and read them. I was without words how the Lord inserted them into this journey. Enjoy!

Therefore comfort one another with these words.
(1 Thessalonians 4:18)

Therefore, the best way to know His voice is to get to know Him. Spend time in His Word, the Bible, and after time, you will be able to understand God's intentions for you and follow His steps. (unknown)

In all your ways acknowledge Him, and He shall direct your paths. (Proverbs 3:6)

Life is full of narrow channels to navigate. We cannot afford to drift away from God and His Word. Only He can bring us through safely.

Listening to God is essential to walking with God. (Charles Stanley)

The Lord is available every hour. He protects us in jeopardy, forgives us during lapses, strengthens us for His service, and is available to us for all time, moment by moment. Find Him while He is still available to be found. (David Jeremiah)

Begin each day alone with God in His Word and in prayer, listening as He speaks to your heart. Believe what He says in Scripture, apply it to your life, and then share with someone else what He has revealed. Be bold and remember that the authority of your message comes from Him. (Charles Stanley)

Unwavering commitment to trust the Lord in all situations is a cornerstone of unshakeable faith. (Charles Stanley)

God is at work in our lives, even when we're being pressured or persecuted for our faith. Don't be intimidated by the world, be motivated by the Word! (David Jeremiah)

Talk to God as a friend, share your most inner thoughts with Him. God cares about you, and He's interested in what concerns you, but you will miss His blessings if you refuse to open your heart to Him fully. (Charles Stanley)

Be of good courage, and He shall strengthen your heart; all you who hope in the Lord. (Psalm 31:24)

The Lord uses testing as a tool to ensure us that if we trust in Him, His thoughts for us are peace and not of evil and that He allows for a time of testing, not to destroy us, but to establish us. (David Jeremiah)

God never promises us an easy time, just a Samuel feeling arrival. (unknown)

Our purpose is to love the Lord and care for one another. Let's be about the Father's business. (unknown)

Our obedience to God's commandments demonstrates our love for Him. (David Jeremiah)

Every day your Bible is getting dirty means that your heart is getting clean! (Charles Stanley)

If you don't love Jesus more today than yesterday, you must be backsliding! (unknown)

We are not responsible for how a person accepts the truth. It's our duty to reveal it. (unknown)

Take courage and obey Him in teaching His truth. You are His messenger to those who need it most, and just as He did for Paul, He will make you victorious in your labors. (Charles Stanley)

Lead me in Your truth and teach me. For You are the God of my salvation, on You I wait all the day. (Psalm 25:5)

Lord, tune my ears so that I may hear Your soft gentle words. (unknown)

The highest honor a man can receive from God is to be His loyal servant. (unknown)

Friend, don't look at your circumstances or try to cut corners. Do your best wherever God places you and trust Him to lift you up wherever you are. Work with excellence and trust He will lead you on the path of blessing. (Charles Stanley)

Do not simply allow Scripture to enter your eyes, but take hold of it so it will rule your heart. (Charles Stanley)

God will be our God, and we must be His people, going where He sends us and speaking whatever He tells us, regardless of visible results. (David Jeremiah)

If you desire to become all that the Father created you to be, you must fill your mind with His ways and principles from His Word. This may appear difficult, but it's the most rewarding endeavor you will undertake, because through it, you will know Him better and experience life at its very best. (Charles Stanley)

Our good Shepherd knows what's around the next turn, and He will never lead us astray. He guides us in one-day increments, and His plans are sealed with His blessings. (David Jeremiah)

If we have no joy in our lives, we must have a leak in our Christianity! (unknown)

To know the Bible is to know God! (unknown)

Examine yourselves as to whether you are in the faith. Test yourselves. (2 Corinthians 13:5)

For the promise is to you and to your children, and to all who are afar off, as many as the Lord our God will call. (Acts 2:39)

We must focus on the living Word of God and allow the Holy Spirit to apply it to our lives. The Bible is the key to the transformation of the mind. (unknown)

Every "you shall not" in the Bible is a promise of God's protection. He is not preventing you from enjoying life, rather He is saving you—keeping you from destroying yourself. (Charles Stanley)

Whoever is wise will observe these things and they will understand the loving kindness of the Lord. (Psalm 107:43)

But be doers of the word, and not hearers only, deceiving yourselves. (James 1:22)

Witnessing is not a matter of eloquence or talent. It's an overflow of the personal relationship with Jesus Christ that is conforming you to His image. As you allow the Holy Spirit to increasingly express His life and power through you, contagious joy will be the fruit of His indwelling presence. (Charles Stanley)

God's ultimate providence over our lives places us where He wants us and when He wants us there. Each of us is born at the exact moment in time that God has ordained. Our times are in His hands; we are here on this earth for a reason. (David Jeremiah)

To him who overcomes, I will grant to sit with Me on My father's throne, as I also overcame and sat down with My father on His throne. (Revelation 3:21)

Ask the father to use you mightily as His representative to those around you. And then watch as He uses His Word to work miraculously through you. (Charles Stanley)

In Him and through faith in Him we may approach God with freedom and confidence. (Ephesians 3:12)

Therefore, brethren, be even more diligent to make your calling and elect on sure, for if you do these things you will never stumble for so an entrance will be supplied to you abundantly into the everlasting kingdom of our Lord and Savior Jesus Christ. (2 Peter 1:10–11)

Remind them to be subject to rulers and authorities, to obey, to be ready for every good work, to speak evil of no one, to be peaceable, gentle, showing all humility to all men. For we ourselves were also once foolish, disobedient, deceived serving various lusts and pleasures, living in malice and envy, hateful and hating one another. But when the kindness and the love of God our Savior toward men appeared, not by works of righteousness which we have done, but according to His mercy, He saved us, through the washing of regeneration and renewing of the Holy Spirit, whom He poured out on us abundantly through Jesus Christ our Savior, that having been justified by His grace we should become heirs according to the hope of eternal life. (Titus 3:1–7)

No matter what limitations you may have, God will use anyone who believes in Him to fulfill His purposes. He does not judge our ability by the world's standards but by His own abilities—which are limitless! (unknown)

Be careful that a man not put his trust in another man's word. Only God has the answers. Trust in Him and His Word, the Holy Bible. (unknown)

The words of the Lord impart strength for every burden, insight for every decision, and a beam of sunshine for every dark day. (David Jeremiah)

A day without Scripture is a day when we are in danger of forgetting the divine Word of encouragement addressed to us. The Lord uses certain verses from the Bible to strengthen our minds every hour of every day. The Bible is the most encouraging book ever written. (David Jeremiah)

You will seek Me and find Me when you search for Me with all your heart. (Jeremiah 29:13)

Casting all your anxiety on Him because He cares for you. (1 Peter 5:7)

The Lord takes pleasure in those who hope in His mercy. Every person who places their hope in Him will never be disappointed. (John Hagee)

The same grace that allowed you to be saved is also now building you up and keeping you from falling. Thank God for His never-ending grace and mercy. (David Jeremiah)

O Lord of hosts, blessed is the man who trusts in You! (Psalm 84:12)

From the government to education, deception has crept in to distort and deceive. Truths that once seemed so evident have been discarded. Even in our churches, pastors are more interested in comfort than the conviction of the Holy Spirit. Jesus declared that God's Word is truth, and the truth will set you free. (John Hagee)

The Savior wants to use your life as a platform for His power. So when He calls, don't worry about whether you're smart, talented, or beautiful enough. Just obey Him wholeheartedly, and He will surely magnify Himself through you. (Charles Stanley)

But none of these things move me, nor do I count my life dear to myself, so that I may finish my race with joy, and the ministry which I received from the Lord Jesus, to testify to the gospel of the grace of God. (Acts 20:24)

He will do the same for you. When you abide in Him, He gives supernatural energy to accomplish the things He requires of you. His Spirit does for you what you cannot do for yourself. (Charles Stanley)

He shall give His angels charge over you, to keep you in all your ways. (Psalm 91:11)

We, like Elijah, should live with confidence in chaotic times, for we are protected by the invisible armies of the Lord of hosts. (David Jeremiah)

Do not fall prey to the lies of the enemy. To the ends of the earth, to the ends of this age, the Lord is with you. (John Hagee)

Commit your works to the Lord, and your thoughts will be established. (Proverbs 16:3)

This is the compilation of quotes I received over the past months. I have them written in my journal, and the Lord had me put them in this section as He commanded.

The law of Your mouth is better to me than thousands of shekels of gold and silver. (Psalm 119:72)

I will instruct thee and teach thee in the way which thou shalt go. I will guide thee with Mine eye. (Psalm 32:8)

The Ending Is Better Than the Beginning

As the days passed and I continued my daily writing, I was constantly adding verses to my journal, still not knowing yet that I would be using them as the Lord places each one in this book. I was still writing this message out when the Lord gave me the instructions to move forward with this book. I was trying so hard to do the Lord's will that I was at one point writing in three different books at the same time. The Lord had to finally tell me to slow down and work on one word at a time.

When I was first starting this journey, I did not think I was doing enough for the Lord. I was worried that I was not meant for this and almost gave up. And that's what the enemy wants us all to do. Then one day, the Lord revealed this verse to me: "Wait on the Lord, be of good courage, and He shall strengthen your heart. Wait, I say, on the Lord" (Ps. 27:14)

That verse opened my eyes, and the Lord told me not to fear or worry. What I was doing every time I went out and visited with people, I was doing exactly what He was asking of me. I was planting the seed and not even realizing it. The Lord comforted me that day, for sure. He only wants the very best for all of us.

> For we walk by faith, not by sight. (2 Corinthians 5:7)

> However, when He, the Spirit of Truth, has come, He will guide you into all truth. (John 16:13)

Like I wrote earlier, I was in the process of writing out this message when I received instruction to go ahead with the book. As I began writing this book, I finished my message: "The Ending Is Better Than the Beginning."

This message was given to me over a couple of months. I had already had the verses written in my journal. I have not counted them all, but I am guessing I have probably five hundred or more in my journal. I still add as the Lord reveals them to me.

In this message, the Lord had me concentrate on the ending of the story and how it will be so much better than the beginning. Hopefully, it will explain how the Lord has already prepared everything for those who put their trust in Him.

> After he had patiently endured, he obtained the promise. (Hebrews 6:15)

> If My people who are called by My name will humble themselves and pray and seek My face, and turn from their wicked ways, then I will hear from heaven, and will forgive their sin and heal their land. (2 Chronicles 7:14)

> And we know that all things work together for good to them that love God, to them who are the called according to His purpose. (Romans 8:28)

> The Lord is not slack concerning His promise, as some count slackness, but is longsuffering toward us, not willing that any should perish, but that all should come to repentance. (2 Peter 3:9)

> Knowing this first, that no prophecy of Scripture is of any private interpretation, for prophecy never came by the will of man, but holy men of God spoke as they were moved by the Holy Spirit. (2 Peter 1:20–21)

And do this, knowing the time, that now it is high time to awake out of sleep, for now our salvation is nearer than when we first believed. (Romans 13:11)

I am the Lord, I do not change, therefore you are not consumed, O sons of Jacob! (Malachi 3:6)

Indeed we count them blessed who endure. You have heard of the perseverance of Job and seen the end intended by the Lord—that the Lord is very compassionate and merciful. (James 5:11)

You therefore, beloved, knowing this beforehand, be on your guard so that you are not carried away by the error of unprincipled men and fall from your own steadfastness. (2 Peter 3:17)

This is a faithful saying, and these things I want you to affirm constantly, that those who have believed in God should be careful to maintain good works. These things are good and profitable to men. (Titus 3:8)

Therefore, brethren, be even more diligent to make your calling and election sure, for if you do these things you will never stumble, for so an entrance will be supplied to you abundantly into the everlasting kingdom of our Lord and Savior Jesus Christ. (2 Peter 1:10–11)

Fear not! For it is written! In My Father's house are many mansions, if it were not so, I would have told you. And if I go and prepare a place for you, I will come again and receive you to Myself, that where I am, there you may be also. And where I go you know, and the way you know. (John 14:2–4)

Be sure of this, I am with you always, even to the end of the age. (Matthew 28:20)

For I am not ashamed of the gospel of Christ, for it is the power of God to salvation for everyone who believes to the Jews first and also for the Greek. For in it the righteousness of God is revealed from faith to faith, as it is written. "The just shall live by faith." (Romans 1:16–17)

But the Lord said to me, "Do not say I am a youth", for you shall go to all to whom I send you, and whatever I command you, you shall speak. (Jeremiah 1:7)

We are not responsible for how a person accepts the truth; it's our duty to reveal it.

Therefore, settle it in your hearts not to meditate beforehand on what you will answer, for I will give you a mouth and wisdom which all your adversaries will not be able to contradict or resist. (Luke 21:14–15)

And He said. My presence will go with you, and I will give you rest. (Exodus 33:14)

Oh, how I love Your law! It is my meditation all the day. (Psalm 119:97)

For the word of God is living and powerful, and sharper than any two-edged sword, piercing even to the division of soul and spirit, and of joints and marrow, and is a discerner of the thought and intents of the heart. And there is no creature hidden from His sight, but all things are naked, and open to the eyes of Him to whom we must give an account. (Hebrews 4:12–13)

For You are my rock and my fortress, therefore, for Your name's sake, lead me and guide me. (Psalm 31:3)

Being confident of this very thing, that He which hath begun a good work in you, will perform it until the day of Jesus Christ! (Philippians 1:6)

The Lord will fight for you, and you shall hold your peace. (Exodus 14:14)

But as it is written: "Eye has not seen, nor ear heard, nor have entered into the heart of man the things which God has prepared for those who love Him." (1 Corinthians 2:9)

For My thoughts are not your thoughts, nor are your ways My ways, says the Lord. For as the heavens are higher than the earth, so are My ways higher than your ways, and My thoughts than your thoughts. (Isaiah 55:8–9)

You may not understand why the Lord directs you on a certain path, but if you are willing to obey Him and learn His ways, you will gain insight into His heart. Then His Spirit will enable you to carry out all the good works He has planned for you to accomplish even before you were born. (Charles Stanley)

All Scripture is given by inspiration of God, and is profitable for doctrine, for reproof, for correction, for instruction in righteousness, that the man of God may be complete thoroughly equipped for every good work. (2 Timothy 3:16–17)

"You are My witnesses," says the Lord, "and My servant whom I have chosen, that you may know and believe Me, and understand that I am He." (Isaiah 43:10)

None of the wicked will understand, but those who are wise will understand. (Daniel 12:10)

With God, all things are possible!

Call to Me, and I will answer you, and show you great and mighty things which you do not know. (Jeremiah 33:3)

It shall come to pass, that before they call, I will answer, and while they are still speaking, I will hear. (Isaiah 65:24)

The Lord God has given me the tongue of the learned, that I should know how to speak a word in season to him who is weary. He awakens me morning by morning. He awakens my ear to hear as the learned. (Isaiah 50:4)

Trust in the Lord with all your heart, and lean not on your own understanding, in all your ways acknowledge Him, and He shall direct your paths. (Proverbs 3:6)

Now, we have received not the spirit of the world, but the Spirit who is from God, that we might know the things that have been given to us by God. These things we also speak, not in words which man's wisdom teaches, but which the Holy Spirit teaches, comparing spiritual things with spiritual. (1 Corinthians 2:12–13)

But blessed are your eyes, for they see, and your ears, for they hear, for assuredly. I say to you that many prophets and righteous men desire to see what you see, and did not see it, and to hear what you hear, and did not hear it. (Matthew 13:16–17)

The Lord is with you, you mighty man of valor! (Judges 6:12)

He shall give His angels change over you, to keep you in all your ways. (Psalm 91:11)

You have made known to me the ways of life. You will make full of joy in Your presence. (Acts 2:28)

And in Your Book they all were written, the days fashioned for me, when as yet there were none of them. (Psalm 139:16)

For whatever things were written before, were written for our learning, that we through the patience and comfort of the Scriptures might have hope. (Romans 15:4)

The end of a thing is better than its beginning, and the patient in spirit is better than the proud in spirit. (Ecclesiastes 7:8)

Forgetting those things which are behind, and reaching forward to those things which are ahead, I press toward the goal for the prize, of the upward call of God in Christ Jesus. (Philippians 3:13–14)

Do you not know that those who run in a race all run, but one receives the prize? Run in such a way that you may obtain it. And everyone who competes for the prize is temperate in all things. Now they do it to obtain a perishable crown, but we, for an imperishable crown. (1 Corinthians 9:24–25)

Therefore, we also, since we are surrounded by so great a cloud of witnesses, let us lay aside every weight, and the sin which so easily ensnares us, and let us run with endurance, the race that is set before us, looking unto Jesus, the author and finisher of our faith, who for the joy that was set before Him, endured the cross, despising the shame, and has sat down at the right hand of the throne of God. (Hebrews 12:12)

But none of these things move me, nor do I count my life dear to myself, so that I may finish my race with joy, and the ministry which I received from the Lord Jesus, to testify to the gospel of the grace of God. (Acts 20:24)

My son, if you receive My words, and treasure My commands within you—then you will understand the fear of the Lord, and find Knowledge of God. (Proverbs 2:1, 5)

This Book of the Law shall not depart from your mouth, but you shall meditate in it day and night, that you may observe to do according to all that is written in it. For then you will make your way prosperous, and then you will have good success. (Joshua 1:8)

My sheep hear My voice; and I know them, and they follow Me. And I give them eternal life, and they shall never perish, neither shall anyone snatch them out of My hand. (John 10:27–28)

Now the Spirit expressly says that in the latter times some will depart from the faith, giving heed to deceiving spirits and doctrines of demons. (1 Timothy 4:1)

Thus saith the Lord unto you, be not afraid, nor dismayed by reason of this great multitude, for the battle is not yours, but God's. (2 Chronicles 20:15)

Commit your way to the Lord, trust also in Him, and He shall bring it to pass. (Psalm 37:5)

Let your heart therefore be loyal to the Lord our God, to walk in His statutes, and keep His commandments, as at this day. (1 Kings 8:61)

Be still, and knew that I am God. I will be exalted among the nations, I will be exalted in the earth! (Psalm 46:10)

It is good for me that I have been afflicted, that I may learn Your statutes. The Law of Your mouth is better to me than thousands of shekels of gold and silver. Your hands have made me and fashioned me, give me understanding that I may learn Your commandments. (Psalm 119:71–73)

Even to your old age, I am He, and, even to gray hairs I will carry you! I have made, and I will bear, even I will carry, and will deliver you. (Isaiah 46:4)

Your ears shall hear a word behind you, saying, "This is the way, walk in it." (Isaiah 30:21)

So then faith comes by hearing, and hearing by the Word of God. (Romans 10:17)

Therefore, comfort one another with these words. (1 Thessalonians 4:18)

For the Lord your God has blessed you in all the work of your hand. He knows your trudging through this great wilderness. (Deuteronomy 2:7)

He who is not with Me is against Me, and he who does not gather with Me, scatters. (Luke 11:23)

I will work a work in your days, which you would not believe though it were told you. (Habakkuk 1:5)

I, even I have spoken, yes I have called him, I have brought him, and his way will prosper. (Isaiah 48:15)

"Because he loves Me," says the Lord, "I will rescue him, I will protect him, for he acknowledges My name." (Psalm 91:14)

In Him you also trusted, after you heard the word of truth, the gospel of your salvation, in whom also, having believed, you were sealed with the Holy Spirit of promise. (Ephesians 1:13)

But sanctify the Lord God in your hearts, and always be ready to give a defense to everyone who asks you a reason for the hope that is in you, with meekness and fear. (1 Peter 3:15)

Blessed is the man whom You instruct, O Lord, and teach out of Your law. (Psalm 94:12)

Beloved, believe not every spirit, but try the spirits, whether they are of God, because many false prophets have gone out into the world. (1 John 4:1)

Now He who has prepared us for this very thing is God, who also has given us the Spirit as a guarantee. (2 Corinthians 5:5)

I will go in the strength of the Lord God. I will make mention of Your wondrous works. (Psalm 71:16)

Come and hear, all you who fear God, and I will declare what He has done for my soul. (Psalm 66:16)

Whatever you do in word or deed, do all in the name of the Lord Jesus, giving thanks through Him to God the Father. (Colossians 3:17)

He reveals deep and secret things, He knows what is in the darkness, and light dwells with Him. (Daniel 2:22)

The Lord is good, a stronghold in the day of trouble, and He knows those who trust in Him. (Nahum 1:7)

And He said, "My presence will go with you, and I will give you rest." (Exodus 33:14)

It is God who arms me with strength, and makes my way perfect. (Psalm 18:32)

For our light affliction, which is but for a moment, is working for us a far more exceeding and eternal weight of glory, while we do not look at the things which are seen, but at the things which are not seen. For the things which are seen are temporary, but the things which are not seen are eternal. (2 Corinthians 4:17–18)

Now may the God of hope fill you with all joy and peace in believing that you may abound in hope by the power of the Holy Spirit. (Romans 15:13)

Go, stand in the temple, and speak to the people all the words of this life. (Acts 5:20)

Therefore, do not be ashamed of the testimony of our Lord, nor of me, His prisoner, but share with me the sufferings for the gospel according to the power of God, who saved us and called us with a holy calling, not according to our works, but according to His own purpose and grace, which was given to us in Christ Jesus before time began. (2 Timothy 1:8–9)

Be diligent to present yourself approved to God, a worker who does not need to be ashamed, rightly dividing the word of truth. (2 Timothy 2:15)

The Lord takes pleasures in those who fear Him, in those who hope in His mercy. (Psalm 147:11)

Open my eyes, that I may see wondrous things from Your law. (Psalm 119:18)

For I say, through the grace given to me, to everyone who is among you, not to think of himself more highly than he ought to think, but to think soberly, as God has dealt to each one a measure of faith. (Romans 12:3)

If a person's beliefs are not in-line with God's Word, then that person best be changing their beliefs. The Word will never change or fail to exist!

Have I therefore become your enemy because I tell you the truth? (Galatians 4:16)

For the promise is to you and to your children, and to all who are afar off; as many as the Lord our God will call. (Acts 2:39)

Before I formed you in the womb, I knew you, before you were born, I sanctified you. (Jeremiah 1:5)

As your days, so shall your strength be. (Deuteronomy 33:25)

Blessed are those who Keep My ways. (Proverbs 8:32)

His Spirit reveals the truth of Scripture to our hearts so that we can learn more about God and His ways. You cannot change yourself—but God can. And once we learn to let Him transform us, we will have the keys to living a truly victorious life. (Charles Stanley)

Not that I have already attained, or am already perfected, but I press on, that I may lay hold of that for which Christ Jesus has also laid hold of me. (Philippians 3:12)

God has chosen the foolish things of the world to put to shame the wise and God has chosen the weak things of the world, to put to shame the things which are mighty. (1 Corinthians 1:27)

You (Israel) are My battle-ax and weapon of war; for with you, I will break the nations in pieces, and with you I will destroy kingdoms! (Jeremiah 51:20)

I am the Alpha and the Omega, the Beginning and the End, the First and the Last. (Revelation 22:13)

Peace I leave with you. My peace I give to you, not as the world gives do I give to you. Let not your heart be troubled, neither let it be afraid. (John 14:27)

You will seek Me and find Me when you search for Me with all your heart. (Jeremiah 29:13)

And you shall be holy to Me, for I the Lord am holy, and have separated you from the peoples, that you should be Mine. (Leviticus 20:26)

I will open the windows of heaven for you. I will pour out a blessing so great you won't have enough room to take it in. (Malachi 3:10)

The Lord has appeared of old to me, saying, "Yes, I have loved you with an everlasting love, there-

fore, with lovingkindness, I have drawn you."
(Jeremiah 31:3)

I am not looking for great and impressive people.
I am seeking the weak, humble servants who put
My Son first so that they may gain strength and
wisdom.

Be careful how you walk, not as unwise men, but
as wise, making the most of your time. Therefore
do not be unwise, but understand what the will
of the Lord is. (Ephesians 5:15–17)

On December 7, the Lord had me write this message: "Be careful when you go out and speak. Many today will judge your words.
Remember what My Word says, that in the last days, many will be
deceived and won't want to hear the truth! Stay strong and keep the
faith. I am coming quickly."

Blessed is the man who listens to Me watching
daily at My gates, waiting at the posts of My
doors. (Proverbs 8:34)

Put your hope in the Lord. Travel steadily along
His path. He will honor you. (Psalm 37:34)

If you reject discipline, you only harm yourself, but if you listen to correction, you grow in
understanding. (Proverbs 15:32)

Faithful is He who calls you, and He also will
bring it to pass. (1 Thessalonians 5:24)

I will instruct you and teach you in the way
which you should go. I will counsel you with My
eye upon you. (Psalm 32:8)

Be watchful, stand firm in the faith, act like men be strong! (1 Corinthians 16:13)

My son, do not despise the chastening of the Lord, nor detest His correction. For whom the Lord loves He corrects, just as a father, the son in whom he delights. (Proverbs 3:11–12)

No temptation has overtaken you except such as is common to man, but God is faithful, who will not allow you to be tempted beyond what you are able, but with the temptation will also make the way of escape, that you may be able to bear it. (1 Corinthians 10:13)

The Lord will fight for you, and you shall hold your peace. (Exodus 14:14)

To him that overcometh will I grant to sit with Me in My throne, even as I also overcame, and am sat down with My Father in his throne. (Revelation 3:21)

Thanks be to God for His indescribable gift! (2 Corinthians 9:15)

You will show me the path of life, in Your presence is fullness of joy. At Your right hand are pleasures forevermore. (Psalm 16:11)

Teach us to number our days aright, that we gain a heart of wisdom. (Psalm 90:12)

For you have need of endurance, so that after you have done the will of God, you may receive the Promise. (Hebrews 10:36)

Being confident of this very thing, that He which hath begun a good work in you, will perform it until the day of Jesus Christ! (Philippians 1:6)

And not only that, but we also glory in tribulations, knowing that tribulation produces perseverance, and perseverance, character, and character, hope. (Romans 5:3,——)

The steps of a good man are ordered by the Lord, and he delighteth in his way.

And the Lord, He is the One who goes before you. He will be with you, He will not leave you nor forsake you, do not fear nor be dismayed. (Deuteronomy 31:8)

God never promises us an easy way, just a safe arrival.

Fearing people is a dangerous trap, but trusting the Lord means safety. (Proverbs 29:25)

Blessed are those who keep My ways. (Proverbs 8:32)

But without faith it is impossible to please Him, for he who comes to God must believe that He is, and that He is a rewarder of those who diligently seek Him. (Hebrews 11:6)

Put your hope in the Lord. Travel steadily along His path, He will honor you. (Psalm 37:34)

Let us therefore come boldly to the throne of grace, that we may obtain mercy and find grace to help in time of need. (Hebrews 4:16)

Nevertheless do not rejoice in this, that the spirits are subject to you, but rather rejoice because your names are written in heaven. (Luke 10:20)

Faithful is He who calls you, and He also will bring it to pass. (1 Thessalonians 5:24)

Let everyone see that you are considerate in all you do. Remember, the Lord is coming soon. (Philippians 4:5)

When wisdom entereth into thine hearty, and knowledge is pleasant unto thy soul, discretion shall preserve thee, understanding shall keep thee. (Proverbs 2:10-11———)

Don't worry about anything, instead, pray about everything. Tell God what you need, and thank Him for all He has done. (Philippians 4:6 NIV)

And you shall know the truth, and the truth shall make you free. (John 8:32)

When thou goest, they steps shall not be hindered. And when you run, you will not stumble. Take firm hold of instruction, do not let her go. Keep her, for she is your life. (Proverbs 4:12–13)

A man's heart plans his way, but the Lord directs his steps. (Proverbs 16:9)

Nevertheless, the solid foundation of God stands, having the seals "The Lord knows those who are His," and, "Let everyone who names the name of Christ depart from iniquity." (2 Timothy 2:19)

The Lord is good, a stronghold in the day of trouble, and He knows those who trust in Him. (Nahum 1:7)

You have made known to me the ways of life. You will make me full of joy in Your presence. (Acts 2:28)

And we are His witnesses to these things, and so also is the Holy Spirit, who God has given to those who obey Him. (Acts 5:32)

Open my eyes, that I may see wondrous things from Your Law. (Psalm 119:18)

The Lord stood with me and strengthened me. The Lord will rescue me from every evil deed, and will bring me safely to His heavenly Kingdom, to Him be the glory forever and ever, amen. (2 Timothy 4:17–18)

Establish Your word to Your servant, who is devoted to fearing You. (Psalm 119:38)

And you will be hated by all for My name's sake. But he who endures to the end will be saved. (Matthew 10:22)

Arise, shine, for your light has come! And the glory of the Lord is risen upon you. (Isaiah 60:1)

For the one who God has sent speaks the words of God, for God gives the Spirit without limit. (John 3:34 NIV)

The Spirit of the Lord God is upon me. (Isaiah 61:1)

Be sure to carry out the ministry the Lord gave you! (Colossians 4:17 NLT)

He who believes in Me, as the Scripture has said, Out of his heart will flow rivers of living water. (John 7:38)

The sheep follow Him because they know His voice. (John 10:4)

Thus says the Lord. Keep justice, and to righteousness, for My salvation is about to come, and My righteousness to be revealed. Blessed is He man who does this, and the son of man who lays hold on it, who keeps from defiling the Sabbath, and keeps his hand from doing any evil. (Isaiah 56:2)

Now may the Lord of peace Himself give you peace always, in every way. The Lord be with you all. (2 Thessalonians 3:16)

For God so loved the world that He gave His only begotten Son, that whoever believes in Him should not perish, but have everlasting life. (John 3:16)

This concludes the written message the Lord revealed to me over about a two-month period. Like I wrote earlier, I was still working on it when I received the *okay* to do this book. Men and women, we are promised so many times by God's own Words that if we believe He is and that His Son, Jesus Christ, came to this earth to save the lost, we will have a guarantee of spending eternity with Him. The bottom line is that we are all born sinners from the beginning of our lives, and if we don't accept the truth, we will perish, separated from God forever. That's why the ending is so much better. When we believe the truth and accept Jesus Christ as our Savior, we are promised eternity with the Lord.

If you are a procrastinator, now is the time to stop! Find the Lord while He may still be found! Tomorrow is promised to no man.

THE FINAL DESTINATION

Now I come to this point in my journey to finish this book. It is by no means the end of my journey with the Lord. Way back on July 1, 2022, the Lord had me write in my journal concerning where He was sending me. He told me, "I am sending you to CW first (CW is Cheyenne Wells, a local town I grew up around) to prove that when I say the days will be like in Noah's time, I am saying that even the people you know will be skeptical of what you are telling them. Stay strong, keep the faith, and finish the race I have put you in. The race will be finished when we meet eye to eye!"

As I look back over time, it is evident that the Lord had plans for me many years ago. I am now able to understand, being taught by the Lord, that He was trying to get my attention when He gave me my letter from Him over twenty years ago. I just didn't know how to listen to Him. Now as I have been on this journey, the Lord has slowly molded me and shaped me into the person He created me to be. When I first started this journey, now over a year, I learned, more than anything, that God is in complete control. Every time I thought I could do something without waiting on Him, it did not work out.

When I finally came to the realization that God created me for this exact time in His master plan, I was able to become a better listener. And like Charles Stanley's quote, and I have it on my wall, *listening to God is essential to walking with God*. The Lord will reveal His thoughts to each of us in His own way.

That's why I truly believe that we are all on our own track meet. We are a team as the "church," but we are responsible for our own actions.

Men and women, we need to be watchful in all things. The world is being set up for the coming of the antichrist and the one-world system. A person has to know the truth, and the only way to know the real truth is to read the Bible and diligently seek the Lord with all your heart.

During this journey, I can honestly say that I have shed so many joyful tears. The Bible says that the Lord gathers both joyful and sorrowful tears and collects them in a bottle. When I finally came to an understanding of the truth, the scales were removed from my eyes. I do now know how much the Father loves each and every one of us. On August 24, 2022, the Lord revealed to me: "I am at work in you! The test will become your testimony, and the battle will become your victory!" As I look back on this journey, it has been an endurance test, for sure. I believe that once the Lord saw that I was and am dedicated, He revealed so much. I am here as a witness to all the words that are written in this book that the Lord was 100 percent in control. I would only write when the Lord gave me the words. I have never had dreams or visions throughout this journey. I would get the thought in my conscience and write it down in my journal.

For me, personally, I am doing what the Lord created me to do. And my ultimate goal is to hear the words from Jesus Himself: "His Lord said to him, 'Well done, good and faithful servant, you were faithful over a few things. I will make you ruler over many things. Enter into the joy of the Lord'" (Matt. 25:21).

God bless everyone who reads these words; these are the words from God through the Holy Spirit. I was just the tool to fulfill His will. To sum it all up, the Lord is saying: "Get prepared, not scared, because the ending is better than the beginning."

> He who testifies to these things says, "Surely I am coming quickly." The grace of our Lord Jesus Christ be with you all. Amen. (Revelation 22:20–21)

REFERENCES

Charles Stanley, In Touch Ministries
David Jeremiah, Turning Point Ministries
John Hagee, Hagee Ministries

Scripture References
New King James Version, NKJC
New King Translation, NLT
New International Version, NIV

About the Author

B ill Hilgemann was born in Sturgis, South Dakota, on November 8, 1964. They moved to Arapahoe, Colorado, in August of 1978. He went to school there, and after high school, he went to work in the oil field. He was married young, which did not work out, and raised his two boys. He currently still resides in Arapahoe.